The Tears of Love.

Ilayaah Kalds Said

Sweden: Ilaryaah AB.

Copyright © 2022 Ilayaah Kalds Said

ISBN: 9798378712090
Available as an electronic book.
Cover and book design by Ilayaah Kalds Said.

DISCLAIMER

This book is a poetry memoir. It reflects the author's present recollections of experiences over time. Some characteristics have been changed, some events have been compressed, and some dialogue has been recreated. This book deals with mental health disorders, domestic violence and heartbreak. While the author has taken great lengths to ensure the subject matter is dealt with compassionately and respectfully, it may be troubling for some readers. Discretion is advised.

DEDICATION

For each piece of our heart that has fallen apart.
By loving those who can't love.
By losing those who loved.

CONTENTS

THE TEARS OF LOVE

I'll tell you how the sun rose;
How the velvet grass was so light and green,
How the field colors were too bright for my eyesight.
Then, I saw you.
You were not following the shine;
The shine followed you.
You just won your race, stuck in a crowd...
Unknown that I was watching you.
I didn't plan to, but then our eyes met.
You were too stunned to speak.
As you walked out, your Father was waiting at the gate.
Telling you to follow him home.
You begged him to let you walk alone;
As you begged, he let you.
I continued walking through the soft music of the meadow.
As I left, I lost sight of any other human being.
Knowing that the next time I turn my head back,
You will follow me.
Then I glanced and saw you;
I ran in laughter and you ran after me.
Across the brown trail, our happiness flode.
Till you finally caught me, the first thing I uttered was:
"How are you" with a melodious tone.
Our smile wouldn't leave as we spake.
Till we came to the end of the gates of paradise.
You said "Be patient, I'm always with you"
Confused, I woke up in my bed.
Real life was still not back in my head.

Let me walk you through the prison of lessons:
Lessons we cannot escape.
Life that we cannot be taught.
Hearts that cannot unbreak.

22.54

Depression has surrounded me for days,
Lord, do not abandon us from your grace.
I look up with eyes of fear.
I lift my hands up hoping you will hear.
A silent heart and a moving lip.
An absent soul and a body that won't shut down.
I direct my blur vision to heaven and ask
"How can you be so merciful but your creations,
so judgemental and hateful?"

23.20

As I finished praying,
Took off the headscarf,
Wiped the tears streaming down like a flood in hurry,
Opened the door,
And walked to sleep
Like nothing ever happened.

23.25
I often wonder if I'm here to live or to slowly die.
My soul is truly satisfied with suffering,
I am closer to dead than alive.
I count of those who rest two meters under the ground.
I witnessed too many long dark nights,
Even longer than the night I was born.
I have forgotten that the morning still exists.
That it shines after the storm.
I fit everywhere at the same time I don't.
I am like them all but I'm not.
I became a lost sheep between lost farmers.
I lost the key to a lost garden.

Alas, lost has always been my middle name.

May I ask you,
Will I ever find peace?

Time may heal all wounds,
but wounds leave scars.
I don't want to be reminded.

A LETTER TO MY BROKEN HEART

———

May I ask,
have you ever loved someone so much
that you worry about their afterlife?

I have.

06.03
As each thing has an end.
That morning light turned to night.
Two injured doves hiding behind chirps.
Inexplicable for poetry.
Indescribable for human nature.
We reached the highest love,
Till we didn't.
A heart shattered into pieces.
We gave them the greatest treasure of all life,
We gave it for free.
Unsure if we should laugh or cry?
We both knew this was the last twinkle of each other's eyes.
We both knew we might never sit with one another again.
Well, he knew,
I couldn't believe him till
I never heard from him ever again.
The clock passed its time, it was time for him to go.
It was the day the perfect lovers went from the label,
Known to unknown.
From love to loved.
From loved to hated.
From the present to the past.
From life to death.

It was the day I realized
that loving someone isn't enough.

07.00
Love cannot be bought.
It has the power to untie every knot.
It is the soul's embracing.
Love might blind you with tears
Walk you miles without shoes,
In an unclear direction and eventually
You will fall and if someone catches you or not
Is the only time you will know
If it is real love.

07.03
When you pass that infinity of love,
You fear,
Fear losing them,
Fear becoming strangers again,
Fear of acting like you two never loved.

07.05

All I could hear was:

"You need to let go of what you love, because you love it"

"I need to let you go"

His last word.

His last time to be seen.

But his voice is still in this theme.

Betrayal and reality crashed,

This feeling isn't unknown to me.

His pureness was unknown to me.

He was what I couldn't imagine finding once in this life.

We were the definition of happiness itself.

One night, it was taken away from our hands.

Powerful became powerless.

It's like a wound in the heart.

Not a wound made by human hands.

Nor could any soul cure me.

For we cannot sew what our eyes don't show.

This is the tragedy they don't know.

07.10

One loving sight turns
To one loving story
Turns to change.
Some days,
My happiness was as the birds that were fed.
On other days,
Loving you was like a bird chasing the wind.

07.15

Indeed, comfort lies in those souls,

Who wish nothing but love upon our hearts.

Blessed are they who findeth,

Someone who has prayed all their life to find them.

07.23

7 billion smiles, but yours was original.

They offered me roses and money,

But your time was valuable.

We shared the most precious seconds in my life.

You provided me with the most profound love

For any humankind.

You took out the amorist in me and the comfort remained.

You encouraged me to laugh and speak when I felt pain.

You enable me to experience years of lost childhood

In only some months.

Wasn't it enough?

07.30
I used to tell him every detail of my day.
I still do, although now is his response
Only a part of my imagination.

09.20

Quintessence of love,

Was I made of your ribs?

The day we met,

Was the clearest sign of kismet.

Our last week was the clearest sign of kismet.

Mind-blowing,

Our journey from day one to the last one.

Miraculous,

How the sun and the moon combined into one.

Only loving sights,

Ignoring that one was land and one the sea.

07.35

My lover's heart was humble and virile.

My lover's love was pure and consistently soft in my vicinity.

In his eyes, was clear happiness and existence found.

I fell over and over again and remaineth unharmed.

A bond like a museum full of art.

The deepest affection,

Yet was never our bodies connected.

An unbreakable force,

Connected by only our spirits.

Two souls seeking fair infatuation in an unfair world.

Love that grew so high,

Till it wasn't reachable for the rest.

Till only death could tear us asunder

In recent times,
You have been in my prayers.
Not to keep you.
Neither to make you love me enough to fight.
I prayed for us to see each other's truth.
I prayed for you to open your eyes and welcome your heart.
I prayed for you to get home safe,
Every straw of hair unharmed.
I prayed for you to reach your deepest goals
With or without me of course.
I prayed for your happiness to glow, even brighter than mine.
I prayed for you to be set free, so you could heal and grow.

But still,
God's answer to me was no.

08.00

Their eyes have not witnessed the beauty I saw in you.

Their heart has not felt what I felt for you.

May it be time for a secret to be shared.

A word that might never be heard.

To take your last name wasn't my dream,

Rather my deepest prayer.

Day and night, I set my face toward the ground and ask:

"If we aren't meant to be in this life please let us be in the next one"

Each word has its own pain,

Each word is its own burden.

I askedst for what I now cannot see.

Your name is kept, hoping for the day,

To freely hold your hands in paradise.

For there would our love be even better,

There would we remain forever,

Yet together.

But did you believe I could enter Heaven?

08.20

I was told we were the ones in the movies.
The ones who meet the right one but at the wrong time.
The ones who wrote the right scripts but the wrong line.
Sorrowful how our desires lie in their highest form.
Truth is, true love will always remain timeless.
Although this truth is not often spoken about.

08.40

It does torment my heart,
How some stories will remain incomplete,
Still beautiful and sweet.

08.36

I truly wish you didn't have to go.
I keep looking at your gifts in my room.
I left each spot where we used to meet.
I wish your last part wasn't a chapter in my book.
I wish others' beliefs weren't in control of our future.
I wish we were older, and you more mature.
I wish you were the one written for me.

I wish I had more lessons without heartbreak.

09.00

You remain the colors of my eyes.

Do not integrate with their lies.

Two spirits, written to be connected,

No accident, nor coincidence.

If two plugs don't match, they can't click.

A battle for two people but only one soldier.

It was hard to fight alone.

One leaving and one holding the sword.

08.30

You know the tragedy deeper than I.

The tragedy that you deny.

Till the truth was revealed.

The chances of marrying one another,

Statistically nonexistent.

Our chances of seeing each other ever again,

Statistically impossible.

Chances of you changing,

Statistically low.

Two lovers keeping hope

Till hope was taken away.

Two lovers controlled by a culture where "love" is unknown.

Beloved, I wish to say that it was us against the world,

Sadly, it was the world against us.

09.10

Although he taught me gratitude.

To not shed tears because it's over.

To smile because of what I have seen.

I have found what earth has been searching for in decades.

09.15

Experiencing genuine love once is

worth more than a million crowns.

Impossible to grab, you feel it.

Impossible to clarify it, only the two of you see it.

I found rare love;

Love not based on looks,

Nor dates in need of money.

Nor talks based on status or carrier.

His past was insignificant to me and so was mine to him.

Indeed, we loved with every cell of our hearts.

Yet we still love even if we are apart.

Alike the trees growing apart,

But under the soil,

They will find their roots attached.

09.19

He said that he was amazed that I saw him.
But how can I not see what is meant for me?

09.25
One may be overpowered.
Two can lift each other up.
I use to tell him "we are stronger together than apart"
But never did I know how strong my heart was
Until I lost my most beloved gift in life,
A best friend.

I wish to tell him that,
He was right about my strength.

09.30

Heart-wrenching

How he doesn't know anything of me today.

Truly heart-wrenching

Unaware of how much

He changed my life

When he met me, Loved me and left me.

If he clocked me today,

He would have been so proud.

I won't do anything more than write this book.

I promised God to trust his time and his overall look.

09.40

When his pictures replay in my head,
I laughed as if he was right beside me.
Then I remind myself that
I left him in the hands of God.
Tell me,
What hands are more loving,
More greater,
Safer for him than God's own?

09.50
Then again at times,
It passes my mind.
Confusion,
If he protected me or lied.
Why would he do this to us?
Love blinded me with forgetfulness
It wasn't me.
He said I deserve better.
But did it not pass his mind to become better?

09.52

Life has always been a vale of tears,
But it hasn't gotten any easier since you left
I have been bearing each burden by myself.
Nowhere to call, Nowhere to ask for help.
I asked for you to be careful,
In my heart you were
And my heart you broke.
You broke me.
You broke yourself.
You broke us
In the very end.

09.57

I told them,

He doesn't know what he is doing

He says he needs to do this for my best.

"Please talk to him."

"Please tell him that he will let us go."

Foolish young girl,

He knew he would be leaving us in the past.

Our final decision was in his own hands.

I hope his decision was worth it.

Worth every loss that came with it.

Sometimes a broken heart
Is the only thing
That can save you from more pain.

————

10.00

Reality feels like a prison
When I don't allow my mind to wander.
I love daydreaming because that's the nearest I can get to you.
My favorite imagination is the one with your precious smile.
Imprisoned by the past.
Although a prisoner can never free himself.
A million tears,
But not one will ever bring you back.
I knew because I tried.
I'm sorry love,
It's out of my hands.

10.05

I didn't only love,

I adored your heart and character.

You captured my soul,

You were the love of my spirit.

Similar to a bright light passing through a dark room.

A dictionary of emotions was discovered.

Till the day the pen ran out of ink,

I tried to rewrite it but then my pen broke.

When I saw blank pages,

It came to my realization,

"that day" actually was our last one.

Dejection then surrounded me,

For your present was now past.

10.07

Greater is truly the lover
Who has nothing to give but gives you his last.
Rather than he who has everything but gives you a part.

10.10

My blood has run cold.

My eyes refuse to watch you leave.

Memories were once everywhere and now started to blur.

Unwilling to wait for something that might never come.

If you ever cross my path again, please remind me.

Remind me of the hours of laughter.

Remind me of our penniless adventures.

Your face may be forgotten but my heart

Can never forget what it once felt and adored.

10.07

Broken and unknown.

Helpless and hopeless.

Attachment and unfulfilled expectations.

Empty words and eyes alike desert.

10.08

I never wanted perfection

I sought connection

I sought protection

I sought confession

I sought consistency

I sought love but feared the loss.

Whoever seeks to change will find his way.
Whoever doesn't, will find an excuse.

————

10.12

He asked for a forbidden friendship,
I answered no.
He cannot leave,
And also seek me in times of need.
I have been everywhere for him,
But I'm only one.
How can I exist in two places at the same time?

10.20

A tenacious lover,
Cannot force one to love what they aren't ready to care for.
Verity,
Free will gives us a choice to fight or go.
It wasn't anybody's decision but his own.
No matter how much I twist and turn it,
He chose to give up on us.
Therefore, I let him go.

Too many days, I didn't know the difference
Between loving someone and respecting myself.
Between humility and self-hate.
Between patience and knowing when I wasted time.
Between words and actions.
Between connection and chemistry.
Between protective and possessive.
Between jealousy and getting disrespected.
Between insecurity and actual safety.
Between safety and solidarity.
The difference between hope and reality.
Between the perishable and the imperishable existences.

10.30

Distance doesn't separate hearts.

A broken heart is what changes you.

Experience is what shapes you.

He left and might never return.

Like the birds whose wings tell them to turn.

Like the rabbits in the street whose toes tell them to run.

Indeed, he might never return.

10.36

Tears created lessons. Lessons that cannot be untaught.

A heart that cannot unfeel what it once felt.

I sat myself on fire to light dust.

I tried to glue glass that has already been broken.

I can no longer fight for closure.

I can no longer chase unanswered questions.

I can no longer wait for clarification.

I can no longer encourage others while I neglected myself.

I can no longer explain how I want to be treated.

I can no longer expect anything from anyone other than me.

10.40

Love is different, yet always the same.

Love is not secret, it is the secret.

Love is not stressful, it is patient.

Love is neither arrogant nor rude.

Love is kind and pure.

Love does not rejoice in wrongdoing.

Love rejoices with the truth.

Love is not forced, rather it forces us to love.

Love does not envy or boast, it is calm.

Love is not irritable or resentful.

There aren't rules,

There aren't guidelines on loving perfect.

Love bears all things and believes all things,

Hopes all things and endures all things.

Love never fails under any circumstance.

11.00

Earth changes when eyes meet
Reality becomes unrealistic
You told me you will never love like this again;
Never see another woman as you saw me.
Truth is, I knew you will.
It will come a day when you chase a woman's love,
As much as you chased mine.
A day you will laugh at her jokes,
And memorize your own just to see her smile.
A day you will sit for hours in the cold just to hear her voice.
A day you will find her in your dreams and pray for a future.
A day you will receive all your goals and dreams,
But without me by your side to catch you in my arms.
A day you will win an Olympiad, become a well-known athlete.
A day you will move out and feel free, and experience life.
A day you will finish your studies and
Become the one you always wanted to be.
For even if you didn't believe in yourself,
I always did from the start to the very end.

Goodbye,
My other half.

II.10

Appreciation is rare to mankind
Till it becomes what we once had.
We do not create ways to love,
Love creates its own ways to find where it belongs.
No matter the chains that hold it down.
No matter all the doors it conceals behind.
True love does not break.
God saw behind the scenes;
It ended right when it needed to end.
Love is only powerful when it is real,
But false love hurts you more than it heals.

Every relationship you meet can either be lessons or destiny,
Nothing in between.

It may be hard to fully understand, but leaving what doesn't bring you clarity, alignment, and peace always ends better. One of the biggest mistakes we commit today is thinking that a person with good character equals a good life partner. I have always been taught that a good man is one who loves me, comforts me, helps me, is nice, doesn't abuse me, doesn't scream, and so on but a good man, in general, does not mean he will be a good man for you. There is much more than just being good to someone. Maybe they have everything you like but are not committed, are afraid of conflicts, or don't have goals. Then what does all his goodness benefit you? Not every single ability is a dealbreaker. It can be worked on through the relationship although some skills do one need to handle before entering a relationship. If you ever have to force something, know that it will not stay and if you ever have to say something more than twice, know that it will not be fixed. The most important thing after you have understood this is to understand that you should never think you will be on the same page if you don't see effort and actions from the one you love. Some people only want to date you but never marry you.

We can never make someone fight for us, it's on them.

We are not stronger than our predestination.

The grief of a loved woman
Who forces a man's hand to let go.
The grief of a man who is forced
To walk away from the gasoline of his heart.

One of the greatest tragedies of all time,
Is forcefully using your free feet to walk in a direction
Away from the love of your life.

23.54
How do I bring it to an end?
The voices that constantly replay in my head?
Eight years old when my eyes first witnessed her,
Lying on the floor half dead.
Our "protector" couldn't control his hands.
Ten years old when we saw him use the knife instead.
Seventeen years old when we found that this wasn't love.

00.01

The worst ones are
The one who knows their lord but doesn't fear,
For they will never fear hurting me.
Let me tell you how affection is unknown to me.

When dominance fills the picture, love disappears.
Something pure as love can't cooperate with hatred.

————

00.10

An object, she became
An object of selfish words
An object of selfish needs
Overwhelmed by his lies
Overwhelmed by what he expressed as love.
Engulfed so deeply in herself,
She was too blinded to see.
Painting a dark image with colors.
Drawn with fear. Sprayed with hope.
At last, she added on empty words.
Her visionless eyes,
Too blinded to see.
That salt and sugar look alike
But are set apart by the taste.

00.15

Access to her own body, lost.
His voice bears more power than his hands.
Than her tone. Than his body.
Bitter like the throne he has been sitting on.

Don't talk to him, Don't talk to him, Don't talk to him
Don't be so hard on him, Don't be so hard on him.

Do not pick up the phone!

He will change position faster than her eyes can blink
He is now the victim, She now the perpetrator.

I told you not to talk to him!

A mind that hears and hears
One scar. Two scars. Three scars.
Your heart is now open
For any opinion
For any war
For any burden

00.20

He wanted a strong woman, right?
Just not stronger than him.
He wanted a smart woman, right?
Just not smarter than him.
He wanted an independent woman, right?
Just a woman who is in need of him.
He wanted a confident woman, right?
Just not so confident
That she values her opinion more than his.
He wanted a woman who adores herself, right?
Only if she loves him more than her own eyes can see.

He wanted a woman who can stand up for herself?
But never stand up to him.

00.25

She follows him and marches.

March so far that she lost sight of her.

He wanted her to give,

Give more than the giver can give.

So she gave everything.

She gave parts of her heart

She gave half of her heart

She gave the other half

Her heart is sore

She gave too much in a short period of time.

Overloved.

Overdosed.

She lost herself when he was done.

Still not satisfied.

He left telling her that she changed.

The reality is he left to find another

Strong mountain to climb and break.

Is the war really over or is she not the victim anymore?

In a world where you are able to love everything,
Why don't you leave any love left for yourself?

00.24

You are inexplicable.

Your beauty gleams,

Your shadow brings light to this world.

Your reflection signals peace.

Please, do not let the beliefs of others define you.

Do not let rumors create you.

You own yourself.

You don't own anyone, nothing else.

Oh Beauty,

Do not dig your own hole, an eternal trap.

Manipulated words,

Not by him, by yourself.

00.34

She yarns for consistency
He desired temporary relief.
She yarns for marriage
He desired the taste of you.
He loves to have fun, still, he seeks a virgin.
Walk out the door, leaving you in pain.
You did what you thought would change his mind.
You valued his needs more than your will.
You went out of your way to please him.
In the way was each of your standards,
For a man who didn't have any.
Do not tear, evildoers will taste what they share.

00.36

He cannot lose possession of anything.
But she can lose everything.
Who can we blame?
The world never accepted her
The world never showed her love
The world made her hate her own blood and bones.
Still blame her for mixing real love with empty words.

01.23

Curves value more than her pure soul.
Her mistakes weigh more than her victory.
Her past is worth more than her present.
They condemn her wrongs, her existence.
It hurts their soul to applaud her.
It is a misery to see a woman, not in need of them.
The sorrow, hate that floods through her veins.
Beauty in her eyes persists unseen.
The knowledge she wears does not satisfy them.
They wish for her to leave her own wisdom behind.
Truth is, they see her but choose to value their own needs.

Lord, I'm grateful,

For the one, you are preparing for me and me for him.

Please may he be Godly and secure in prayer.

May he fall out of love with this perishable world.

May he be kind, even if he is walking on air.

May he be strong enough to stand alone and

Humble enough to seek guidance.

May he be big-hearted and able to give with all his heart.

May he be brave but never mindless.

May he be a good listener and a wisdom seeker.

May he know how to ask and receive forgiveness.

May we live with laughter and joy, as well as with patience and peace. Oh, may we be best friends, sharing all of our experiences, growing together, supporting each other, and never judging each other for where we have been or where we will end up.

Amen.

BAD COMPANY RUINS GOOD MORALS

————

Negativity in your life will eventually affect you
even if you have a "strong" personality.

06.00

I knew the betrayal,
He did everything he said he would never do.
He never would do to you.
I knew the betrayal,
Confidants have bestowed me.
I became hateful to them.
All day long, their hatred surrounds me like the ocean,
I am drowning and cannot see land.
Salt is burning my eyes,
I'm near losing my sight.
My loved ones have driven far away from me.
In the place of my confidants, I only find darkness.
I knew the betrayal,
Betrayal has no limits.
We need water to survive,
But even water can sink a ship
When it fills it from the inside.

The sadness of betrayal,
It is never found with your enemies.

06.10

I want you to visualize,
You own a delightfully secluded yard.
Bigger than your eyes can witness.
The garden can hold all your favorite fruit
The juiciest fruit you have ever seen
You have your most lovely roses,
That shine from a distance.
Months, and years of work to build this empire.
One day you witness a small amount of weed growing.
Do you remove it or do you let it grow?
Slowly grow bigger and increase and destroy
All the work you have put in to grow this yard.
Because you feared removing it?

Now imagine if the garden was you.

06.20

Endlessly,
The pain will remain and the scars will not heal.
For the one who keeps watering thorny plants,
You don't owe anyone an explanation
It's your path, your garden with roses.
They are among the weeds
Among the dead flowers.

06.25

Weed is alike a faulty friend;

That friend who informs you about all rumors but

Never taught you to protect your name behind closed doors.

That friend,

The better it goes for you, the less you will hear from them.

Although when you are down,

They'll be the first to call to know and utter

"Sorry, I didn't know, I've been busy".

That friend,

Who claims to love you, still you find them

Side by side with those who hurt you.

That friend,

Who let you swim in hardship

And won't enter the water with you,

Yet they still stand at the finish line

Excited to share the price with you.

You know that friend who only pats your back

to put the knife right back.

You know that loyal helping hand,

Is the same hand that got your shoes stuck in the sand.

06.30

We tend to forget;
Forget how a bit of mold increases over time.
Either you let it break you
Either you let it make you.
Do not make hasty decisions based on temporary problems.
You know, when they treat you as an opinion,
leave them like a choice.

What if you removed the weed
when you first saw it?

07.00
Behind a closed door,
Behind the smile behind my sorrow.
I tell myself; calm down, calm down,
Is it worth it? To let the foolish control you?
The truth is you will always meet the ignorant ones
You will always meet the hateful ones
You will always meet the jealous ones
You will always meet the fake ones
No matter how well you treat others.

Since a human can simply not escape human nature,
Which disappointment is a part of.

07.10

Two communicate,
As long as one speaks they can't hear.
As long as one hears they can't speak.
Bodies created to have two ears yet only one mouth.

07.15

The abundance of the heart the mouth speaks.
How one articulates at all times,
Misery to happiness
Confesses their deepest character.
Only in the tongue you find faithfulness.
They say lying is an evil art,
Painted with temporary color.
The sadness of a liar's destiny,
When he speaks the truth, he is still not believed.
The sadness of those who share what is not meant to be said,
It spreads to everyone.

07.20

Although silence is as difficult as an uncontrolled mouth,
Nor is the silence empty, It is full of answers.
Opinions are limited to what they let you know.
To remain quiet,
Can even make the unwise seem educated.

07.30

Are you unaware,
That righteous company leads to righteous actions?
Are you unaware that knowledge leads to wise decisions?
Ask success, it is familiar with loneliness.
It knows when to choose growth over a false company.
It does not forsake friends or advice, for they are important.
Instead, it seeks the wise ones to grow from.
It guards its circle regardless of any cost.
They let go to grow.

May I ask you,
Do you truly get any peace from the company that you keep?

FORGIVENESS AND WALKING AWAY

———

23.30

Asking for forgiveness
Receiving forgiveness
Accepting forgiveness
Without an apology
Is the most humble level
Your heart can enter.

01.00

Love without forgiveness is alike
The spiritually blind walking near a ditch.
If the eyeless lead the eyeless,
Won't eventually both stumble and fall?
But with an open warm heart,
Won't your sights grow too?
Give up the suffering of the past
That still holdeth your kindred soul back.
When forgiveness is found,
Inner freedom is unlocked.

Insight leads to insight.

21.32

Should he change?

You can't save him.

You can't change him.

You can save your own crown.

You can change your own mind.

21.40

Lessons have taught me,

That we can never teach a man to be a man.

As we can never teach a woman to be a woman.

We do not teach others,

But those who seek change will themselves find a teacher.

01.00

Every soul that unites with yours
Is another lesson. Another tear. Another fear.
Don't let the temptation make a choice
That is familiar to your old, dear.
They offer you to try it till you crave it.
They keep giving you what you crave,
Then threaten to take it away
If you are the one chasing, who is running away?

01.10

A weak flesh, but a willing spirit indeed.
A heart that seeks acknowledgment
A body that strives for peace.
Temptation is a temporary test of intelligence.
Like the desire to swim in the cold sea.
The farther you go from land,
The farther your body goes from your soul.
It leaves.

Bright side:
Abuse is temporary
Hate is temporary
Sadness is temporary
They are temporary
Life is temporary.

02.10

If the night does not sleep, how will the dark?
If the glacier is melting, how can the cold stay forever?
If even the world was once one continent but is now six?

Let all that you do be done in the name of love.

22.00

The world will not harden me.

A world of hatred will not tell me how to love.

Love endlessly,

Love even if it doesn't make sense to others.

Love deeply,

It's okay.

Drive hours to surprise someone.

Insist on following them home.

Leave small love notes before you go out.

Turn off your phone to share a day with someone.

Tell them how much you love them even if it's every day.

Give without expecting.

Say no without rejecting.

It's okay to love.

What leaves you were never there
in the first place.

22.30

Sow seeds of forgiveness,
Reap the fruits of mercy.
Sow seeds of love,
Reap the fruits of fondness.
Sow seeds of hate,
Eat sour grapes.

What you gave away your attention to
Is what ends up overpowering you.

I assure you that you can never change what you did not create. They will forever see, hear, and learn what they want till they don't want to anymore. Forgiveness, patience, gratitude, and sincerity are essential to break the chains of your past. Forgiveness and acceptance go hand in hand because life is simply shaped by what is in our minds. If there is no enemy within, the enemy outside can do you no harm. What is also important to remember is that forgiving somebody does not force you to give them another chance. Forgiveness and acceptance are for your personal peace. Not for theirs, another chance is for them to prove to you. Forgive yourself. Face your shadows or you will continue to see them in others. Verily, I say unto you, the world through your eyes is only a reflection of your inside.

Reminder:

When your reaction does not result in them changing
behavior, will another reaction not change how they treat you.
The only thing you ever will be able to control is yourself.

May I ask you,
How long will you fear leaving them in the past?

SELF LOVE

———

Confirmation is good
But the most important confirmation
will always be our own.

20.30

I'm the seed that grows in the dark

A flower, watered daily in secret.

Till I one day grew so big.

That I could reach the sky with my bare soul.

My leaves were not bigger than I could bear.

My smell did not reach further than I could move.

The flower's charm lies in her seed and the seed created her.

The part she always left out, hoping people will not see.

But why?

Our story is the most beautiful thing we could ever share.

20.32

His loss became my treasure.

Losing him was my breakthrough.

It took me so long to realize

That the love from my own well was far greater than any love

I ever sought from any other source.

I could have spared myself from heartbreak

But then,

Wouldn't I have spared myself from happiness too?

20.35
I inspect the woman in the mirror.
I see a woman who accepted.
I see a woman who learned.
I see a woman who changed for the better.
I see a woman who created her own happiness.
I see a woman who refused to give up.
I see a woman who refuses to stay in the same place.
I see a woman who will applaud herself.
I see a woman who won't escape the dark.

She grew from the dark till she reached the sun.
She embraced the chaos,
Till it colored her life with purpose.
Goddess.

21.00

Keeping faith left her faithless
Do not define her by the culture
Do not emphasize her by clothes
She is not an image of the community.
She is her own soldier, in the war.

21.06

Her name is Arcane.
A flame dressed in angel skin.
A mess and a masterpiece.
If you could count all her tears,
Her sorrow would be named the red sea.

21.10

Each inch of her was perfected.
Every mark,
Every single strand of her hair.
Every soldier received a different power of beauty.
Yet still, they are all created the same.
One was not created of gold and the other one of dust.
How can he not love what he created?

Repeat:
Acceptance is the key,
I love and respect me.

We often let the media decide standards for us,
what is beautiful and what is not. Reality is that the media was
created to blind us from the beauty of reality. Have you ever
taught about how so much was once real and is today false?
How much was once false but today it is real?
What do they know about reality?
Isn't the whole society collecting money on falseness?

22.25

Dear, embrace your beauty;
Time changes,
People change,
Ideals and trends change all the time.
May time give you gray hair
But it doesn't change your features,
We always remain the same.

22.30

They used to hate my kinky hair,
They used to laugh and share.
But how come today, the same people
Are sleeping with braids to wake up with curls?
The same people got a perm at the salon?

22.32

It's beyond their imagination;
Beauty is subjective,
Beauty isn't defined by skin,
Nor the curves of each body.
Beauty is beyond what meets the human eye.
No physical characteristic can be synonymous with beauty.
Beauty is secret but when it's found,
It can never be unseen.

22.34

In the mirror, she gazes.
She exchanged external validation for internal validation,
She found the puissance of her ethereal love,
Her deepest peace. Her long-lost treasure.
She was the partner of her dreams.

22.35

At night, she drowns herself
In unanswered questions of the past.
A past that is no longer present.
She doesn't understand,
Statements have no answers,
Only questions have.

How can you understand the start,
If you haven't reached the very end?

I can't. Why can't I?
I will fix him. Why do I care?
I'm ugly Why do I feel this way?

22.36

Self-love is the missing panacea.

Blessed are the mornings that you wake up.

Your energy is a gift.

Your body is your temple.

Your spirit is your own peace.

22.40

Practice your own love language
By yourself for yourself
Repeat nice things
Do something nice
Take yourself on sweet dates.
Love your body.
Take care of it.
Spoil yourself with gifts.
Don't wait for anyone to be your second half
Be whole by yourself.

22.50

Don't make them commit.
You will fail.
You need to commit dear
Commit to loving yourself
Commit to controlling yourself
Commit to your healing path
Commit to finishing things.

My trainer used to tell me;
"If you give up one time when it is hard,
then you will always give up when it's hard."

To change:

It starts with honesty, what do you feel at this very moment? What do you need to do at this very moment for your happiness? A Part of moderation is recognizing and accepting that we only can change, only can grow to a certain extent in a certain amount of time. It is about identifying what one's priorities are. Start slowly, it's a process to sustain your spiritual health, and heal your emotional wounds.

You are not expected to know everything that you have never been taught, and even if you are required to know something, it will take time for you to learn it. This goes for everything in life, religious practices, relationships, education, self-care, etc. This amount of time will vary from person to person. There is no need to involve unnecessary people in your growth nor to compare with other people's journeys. It is as important to not involve others as it is to not put yourself down for not being able to change as fast as you wish. If you don't find love for yourself before the change has occurred, then you will not find love after you accomplished what you wanted either. Self-love is also leaving what is hurting you and keeping what you love. You cannot stay in an environment that you are trying to outgrow. Search for happiness by yourself no matter what you will lose on the way.

*The secret to your future is hidden in your daily routine;
only six months of intense focus changes years.*

00.00

Haven't you circled the same village long enough?
Turn northward, and continue to walk.
Time will tell the truth.
This storm will end.
Life will surprise you.

I promise you,
Life is much more than a thief.

00.02

When I find life hard,
I remember that once upon a time,
I found it hard to walk.
Now I walk around 5000 to 10000 steps a day.

00.04

What we couldn't do once as a child,
We have taught ourselves now
Children can only succeed
Because they make up barriers
For what seems to be "impossible".

Reminder:

Your dreams aren't too big;
This world's expectations are too small for you.
Keep believing in the unknown;
For there is a lot we haven't seen yet.

May I ask you,
Has God ever tested anyone
without a price waiting at the finish line?

THE PAST

——

When the devil reminds you about your past,
Don't forget to remind him of your future.

02.00

Impossible to grow without water, they said.
Little did we know
I was one of the few flowers
That grows in the desert.
Heatwaves did not kill the flower,
The flower grew through it.
Bigger after every survival.
One day,
Everything worked out.
No obstacle lasts forever.

02.02

Don't we consistently learn and improve from our mistakes?
Then why are we so afraid of committing them?
The biggest mistake is truly the decisions we didn't make.
Although labeling mistakes as mistakes is meaningless.

02.10

I know,
You are trapped between four walls.
Look closely at the walls,
You will see that one of them
Was a door this whole time.

02.20

Acknowledge those who remind you of your past mistakes,
To leave them in the past.
What you have left physically
shouldn't bother you mentally anymore.
How can one's spirit ever rest then?

02.25

Verily, I say unto you
Make peace with your previous,
So it won't disturb your present.
Losses and failure were only there to wake you up,
So you could receive victory.

02.30

The past was the day I was born.

The past was the day I learned to write,

Today I wrote a book.

The past was the day I stumbled over a stone,

Today I went back up.

The past was the day I learned to swim,

Today I saved my life.

The past was the day he left me,

Today I said " I love you" to myself.

The past was the day I hated myself

Today was the day I wrote a book about loving yourself.

02.35

The past created us
We created the future.
Do not fear the unknown,
For the unknown also fears you.

02.40

A young flower,
Spent nights
Begging you to take her,
But you never did.
Broken but did not give up,
Billions of gifts but an answered prayer,
Was the best of them all.

May I ask you,
How long will you keep letting your past stand in the way?

VALUE OF TIME

———

Time can change everything,
It can even shake anchored mountains.

00.00

The more information my mind took in,
The slower the days seemed to pass,
Although each year passed very quickly.
The sun sank and darkness occupied the left ones.
It never said goodbye,
It left the kids with empty words;
Words about us having all our life left.
Look, we are grown-ups now.
Wait, father, brother, beloved, where did you all go?
If you do not fear time,
It will burn you alive till you feel it;
To teach you that the smallest parts remain the biggest ones.
That the clock doesn't sleep.
I should have shared the beauty of their existence in my life.
I should have treated them with loving care.
Sadly,
Value was found after I saw my beloved's empty chair.
We may be powerful today but time
Will always overwin us.

00.31

Oh beloved, time has parted us.
How strange that our time has now faded?
You were a big part of my journey but
I wished for you to be my destiny.
How can my heart give someone else that love?
That love I only wanted to give you.

00.35

If I had the choice,

All success in the world would be exchanged

To feel the love with him once again.

Even if I had to start our journey all over.

For every day of the days we shared was filled with adventures.

A wise man once read me this as a child, He said:
"To understand the value of 40 years,
Ask someone who lost his mother.
To understand the value of 20 years,
Ask a divorced couple.
To understand the value of 10 years,
Ask someone who lost her brother or sister.
To understand the value of one year,
Ask a student who failed in school.
To understand the value of 9 months,
Ask a mother.
To understand the value of one month,
Ask someone who did not pay his rent.
To understand the value of one week,
Ask a journalist.
To understand the value of one minute,
Ask someone who missed the train.
To understand the value of one second,
Ask a person who just avoided an accident.
To understand the value of one millisecond,
Ask a runner who won a silver medal in the Olympics. "

We never bought anything with money,
We bought it all with hours of our time.

00.40

None of your earthly fortunes can bribe the angel of death.
Nor does worrying add a single hour to your light.
For when the end of the candle has passed,
The light goes out,
Smoke rises to the sky.
There we all stand the same,
No body more worthy.
In death, you find no age, gender or faith.
In death, you find no black and white.
In death, you find no yellow or brown.
In death, you find no famous or poor.
Except for the millionaires of positive deeds,
Even richer than the billionaire in cash.
It is okay,
Fear of death is common,
But foolish are they who don't fear death,
For even to a believer is the future unknown.

Eternal rest.

00.45

Every activity under heaven has its own time.

All happiness, a beginning

All suffering, an end.

You are the same, past, present, and future

But with different levels of knowledge and experience.

To understand the value of anything in life.

To understand the value of every moment

To every person at every price.

You need to understand the value of time.

Time is running and we are chasing,

Or are we the ones running and time is chasing us?

00.50

Hours have been lost in worrying
Of what is not in our hands.
Isn't our body more than clothes?
Isn't our brains more than the thoughts of others?
Isn't our desire more than food?
Millions of birds do not sow or reap
Still, God provides them all with nourishment daily.
Millions of seeds do not gather in barns.
Still, He sends rain.

Do you not think human creation is more valuable to God?

If you believe God gave up on you, look again.
If you still breathing, your chance is still there.

When you're alone standing in the dark,
You will see the light much brighter,
To light up your way.
But you won't see the obstacle before you fall on it.
It keeps feeling like sand under your feet,
Till you feel grit deep in your toes,
And blood running out of your shadow.

21.00

Ambrosian when we first eat it,

But leaves a sour aftertaste.

God's eyes see farther than our eyes will ever be able to see.

The almighty taught me the difference.

Between a protection and restriction.

They utter it's a blessing when they sin to get it.

What we choose to put before God will eventually collapse.

21.50

Death stresses them.
I fear death but not of the body.
I fear the death of my heart.
The day I lost the keys to my own heart,
Is the day I will fear myself.
I will no longer be human,
But a wandering body
In a worldly life
Based on illusionary enjoyment.

22.00

One day, they will know that
What one physically owns today,
Will tomorrow own them.
Everything that can be touched
Can be gone in a blink of an eye.
Money disappears,
For the meaning of it is to be used.
New cars become old cars.
Designer clothes become untrendy.
A house is only a temporary place to sleep in.

22.20

What no human can ever take away,
As you are still breathing,
Is what you mentally own,
Such as your wisdom,
Your knowledge,
Your experiences,
Your faith.

May I ask you,
If your death day was tomorrow night,
What would you regret the most?

THE TEARS OF LOVE

23.59

Catch your destiny before it catches you.

Do not wait, do not worry.

Do not sympathize with the lies of the world.

Do not fear people.

In the end, we all share the same blood and last breath.

But never forget to love, even if you fear.

For love will never disappear.

00.00

Thank you, dear

For following me

And reading all to the end.

Life changes faster than we ever could imagine.

Now, when you are closing this book,

I shall be closing it with you.

By the time you have read this book, I shall be 18 years old.

Everything that has happened before is only a lesson.

That is all I wanted to share with you.

Thank you for following my journey marked by these pages.

This is the last they get,
150 pages or less
But not a single one of regret.
Farewell.

THE TEARS OF LOVE

THE TEARS OF LOVE

ABOUT THE AUTHOR

Ilayaah Kalds Said, with Coptic roots, was born and raised in Sweden. She is a poet, author, and full-time athlete. At the age of 16, she started writing "The tears of love" and published it as a 18-year-old. She studies the Social Science Programme in upper secondary school. Ilayaah has been involved in different human rights organizations and their projects. These have affected her views deeply. From a young age, she developed a love for education and shared her learning experiences on Social media. Ilayaah also used her voice to bring attention to important societal issues such as economic inequality, vulnerable groups, and the right to grow up in a safe environment. For the latest news and updates on her upcoming literary works, follow her business account on Instagram: @Ilaryaah.

Printed in Great Britain
by Amazon

23456178R00086